Y0-ELA-496

Ron and Joyce Cave, both senior officials of the
Cambridgeshire Educational Authority,
have written and developed these
books to be read by children on their own.

A simple question is asked about each topic discussed
and is then immediately answered.

A second, more general question follows which is
designed to provoke further thinking by the child
and may require parental assistance.

The answers to these second questions
are found at the end of the book.

Designed and produced by
Aladdin Books Ltd
70 Old Compton Street · London W1
for: The Archon Press Ltd
8 Butter Market · Ipswich

Published in the U.S.A. 1982 by
Gloucester Press
730 Fifth Avenue · New York NY 10019
All rights reserved

Library of Congress Catalog
Card No. 82-81166
ISBN 531 03464 X

Printed in Great Britain

WHAT ABOUT?
RACING CARS

Ron and Joyce Cave

Illustrated by
David West and Paul Cooper

GLOUCESTER PRESS
New York · Toronto

The Racing Car

The scream of powerful engines and the smell of burning oil mean one thing to millions of motor racing fans all over the world – the race is on! For sheer thrills and excitement, no other sport matches motor racing. Grand Prix races are the most popular of all. Grand Prix is French for the "big prize," and top drivers compete in these races to become world champion. But whether they succeed or not depends as much on the performance and reliability of their cars as it does on their own skill and daring.

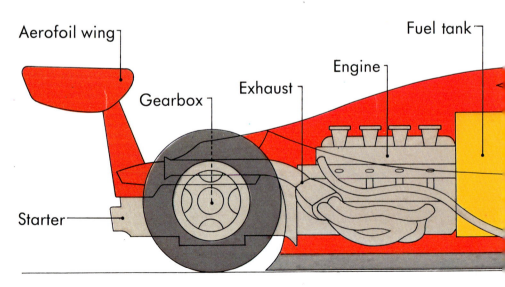

Aerofoil wing

Fuel tank

Engine

Exhaust

Gearbox

Starter

A typical modern racing car is shown below. It has a low, sleek shape which cuts through the air like a knife. Its powerful engine is mounted at the back. Huge, wide wheels grip the racetrack for high-speed cornering. The driver lies well down in the cockpit, which is tailored to fit his body. Aerofoil wings, or "spoilers," are fitted to the front and back of the car to give greater stability. The air rushing over these presses the car firmly down onto the track. These cars can achieve speeds of over 320 kph (200 mph).

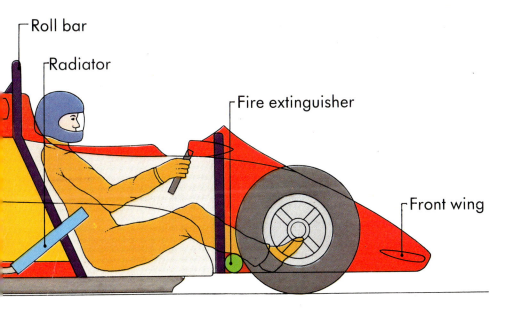

Roll bar

Radiator

Fire extinguisher

Front wing

Early Races

Motor racing began almost as soon as the motor car was invented. One of the first official races was held in France in 1895. It was from Paris to Bordeaux and back, a distance of 1178 km (732 miles). There were 22 entrants, but only nine cars finished the race. The winner was Emile Levassor, driving a Panhard car. His average speed was just 24 kph (15 mph).

What kind of cars entered this race?

There were gasoline, steam and electric powered cars. Of the nine cars that finished, eight were gasoline-driven, and only one powered by steam. By the end of the century, nearly all cars were gasoline-driven.

What fuel do today's racing cars use?

Panhard

First Grand Prix

The first race to be called a Grand Prix was held at Le Mans, in France, in 1906. It was staged over two days, and the drivers had to complete six 103 km (64 miles) laps on each day, in the fastest time overall. The winning car was a red Renault, averaging 101 kph (63 mph). In the following years, racing cars became "monsters" as designers strove to make them faster and more powerful.

Renault

What were these "monsters" like?

The Mercedes of 1914 was the most successful, taking 1st, 2nd and 3rd place in the French Grand Prix. It had an adapted fighter-plane engine.

Mercedes 1914

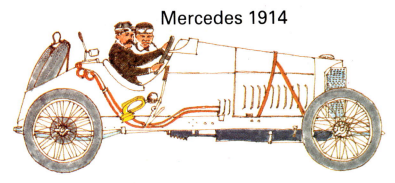

The Fiat "Mephistopheles" of 1909, was built like a tank. Its huge engine gave it a top speed of over 160 kph (100 mph).

When was the first British Grand Prix?

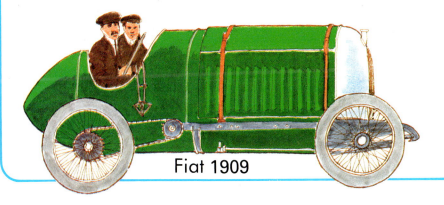

Fiat 1909

Between the Wars

The 1920s and 30s were the great romantic years of Grand Prix racing. There were closely fought battles on the track between firms like Bugatti, Alfa Romeo, Bentley and the German Auto Union and Mercedes. Racing car engines became lighter and more powerful, and improved tires, brakes and suspension made them more reliable. Tazio Nuvolari was the great driver of this period. Many people think that his victory in the 1935 German Grand Prix was the finest driving display ever seen.

Bugatti 1928

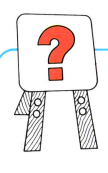

What was so special about this race?

Nuvolari was driving an Alfa Romeo, but the German Auto Union and Mercedes had more powerful cars. Nuvolari's victory was an example of driving skill beating superior engine power.

Can you name any other great drivers of this period?

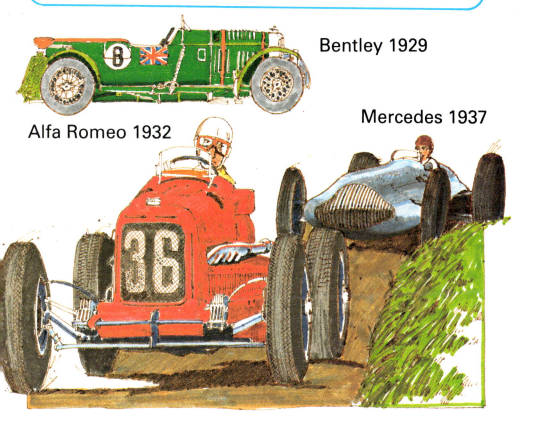

Bentley 1929

Alfa Romeo 1932

Mercedes 1937

Champion Drivers

The Grand Prix world championship for drivers began in 1950. The Argentinian driver Juan Fangio won the championship five times in the seven years from 1951. Italy's Alberto Ascari and Britain's Stirling Moss were other top drivers of this period. Alfa Romeo and Ferrari cars dominated the tracks, and it was not until 1957 that a British car, the Vanwall, won a Grand Prix.

Vanwall 1957

Alfa 1951

How is the world championship won?

The scoring system has been changed a number of times by the Grand Prix authorities. Drivers gain points for finishing in the first six places in a race. The driver who wins most points in the season is the champion.

Can you name any Grand Prix races?

Ferrari 1953

A New Design

In 1962, the Lotus 25 burst onto the Grand Prix scene, winning seven of the ten Grands Prix raced that year. The Lotus 25 was the first modern racing car to have a "monocoque" construction. Monocoque means single shell, with the body and chassis of a car formed from a single unit. All Grand Prix cars today are monocoques, with even the engine and fuel tanks being part of the chassis.

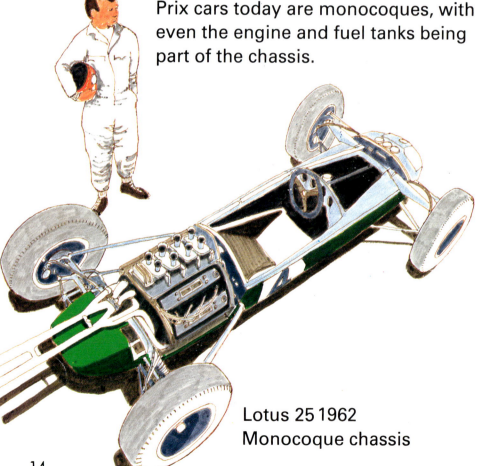

Lotus 25 1962
Monocoque chassis

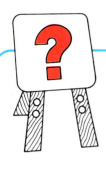

How big is a racing car engine?

At present, Grand Prix rules limit normal engine sizes to 3 liters, and turbocharged engines to 1.5 liters. Cars must not have more than 12 cylinders. You can count the eight cylinders on the 1982 Brabham shown below.

What is a turbocharged engine?

The Big Race

Stop the race

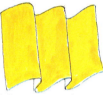

No overtaking

End of the race

A Formula 1 Grand Prix usually has about 24 competitors, and lasts for anywhere from two to four hours. For two days before the race, drivers run timed practice laps. A driver's place on the final starting grid depends on the speed of his fastest practice lap. These placings are important, because the further back in the field a driver is, the more difficult it is for him to win. The best position is called the "pole" – on the inside of the front row for the first corner. The colored flags on the left are used by race officials to give drivers instructions during the race.

What does Formula 1 mean?

Racing cars are divided into different groups, or Formulas. Each Formula has its own rules governing the cars' design and engine size. Formula 1 cars are the most powerful, and race in the Grands Prix.

Can you name other Formulas?

Formula 1 1982

Pit Stop

Pit board

If a driver finds something wrong with his car during the race he pulls into the pits. These are trackside workshops where the team's mechanics wait. Often, the car simply needs more fuel, or a change of tires. But some mechanical faults can put the driver completely out of the race. Pit teams also hold up a board, like the one on the left, when their driver roars past. This tells him his position in the race.

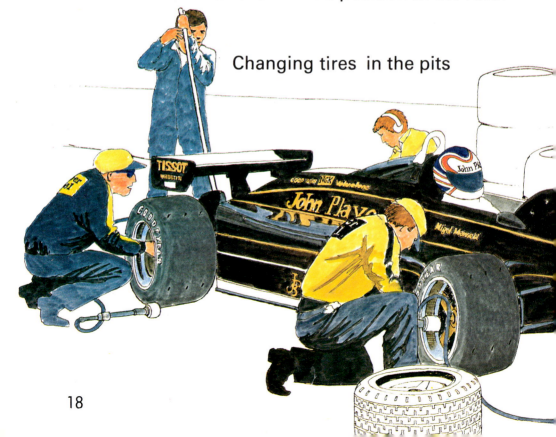

Changing tires in the pits

Why are tires changed in a race?

Different tires are used for wet or dry conditions. Smooth tires, or "slicks," are best for a dry track. Wet weather tires have treads to get rid of rainwater. Pit mechanics can change tires in less than 20 seconds.

How did the pits get their name?

Wet weather tire

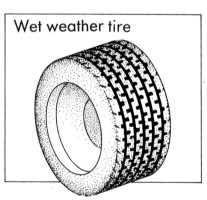

Dry weather tire

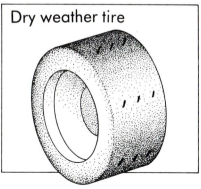

Safety

Motor racing is a dangerous sport, and accidents do happen. Modern cars are designed to protect the driver from the impact of a crash. A roll bar prevents the driver from being crushed if his car turns over, and cars have automatic fire extinguishers. Drivers wear crash helmets, flameproof clothes, and safety belts. Fire marshals are always on hand to rescue drivers if they crash.

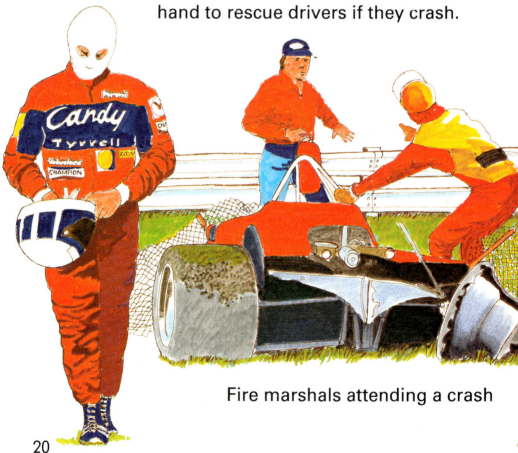

Fire marshals attending a crash

What other safety measures are taken?

On more dangerous parts of the course there are "chicanes" – tight "S" bends that slow the drivers down. A runoff area allows cars to spin-off safely away from other cars. Catch fences and crash barriers absorb crash impacts, protecting both the driver and the nearby spectators.

Why do spectators need protecting?

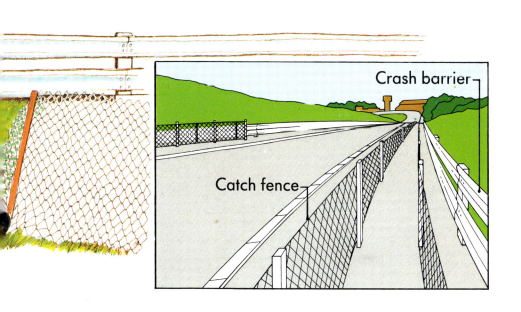

Crash barrier

Catch fence

Can~Am Races

The North American Can-Am (Canadian-American) Challenge Cup races began in 1966, and at first there were no limits on engine size. The rules were changed in 1977, limiting Can-Am racers to a maximum engine size of 5 liters – almost double that of Grand Prix cars. But perhaps the best known of all American races is the "Indy" – the Indianapolis 500.

1979 Can-Am Racer
Budweiser Spyder

How is the Indianapolis 500 run?

It is run over 200 laps of a 4 km (2.5 miles) banked oval track – a total distance of 800 km (500 miles). The pace is fast, with average speeds reaching nearly 320 kph (200 mph), and the "Indy" has been the scene of some terrible and spectacular pileups.

When is the Indianapolis 500 run?

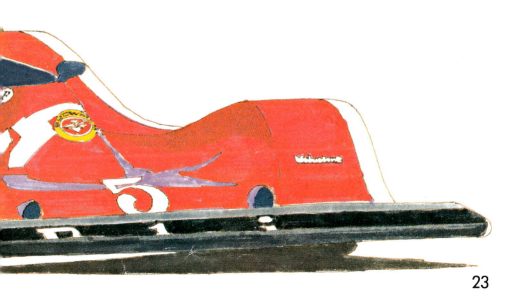

Le Mans

Although Grand Prix racing began at Le Mans, it is now more famous for the Le Mans 24-Hour Endurance race. Le Mans cars have to be based on the ordinary road models sold to the public. But the manufacturers can make considerable changes to improve their cars. The Porsche shown below has a highly-tuned turbocharged engine. Le Mans cars can reach speeds of 320 kph (200 mph). The winning car is the one that travels the greatest distance in the 24 hours.

Do Formula 1 cars race at Le Mans?

No. The Le Mans 24-hour race is for sports cars, not racing cars. Different classes of cars can enter, ranging in power from 1.5 liters to 2.6 liters turbocharged. Prizes are awarded for each class. Each car carries two drivers, who take turns at the wheel.

When was the first Le Mans 24-hour race?

Porsche 956

Future Racers

The racing cars of the future will look very different from the ones of today. New types of races will appear, to keep pace with changes in racing car technology. Illustrated below is a gyroscopically balanced one-wheeled racer of the future. But one thing is certain, motor racing will remain one of the most popular and dangerous of sports.

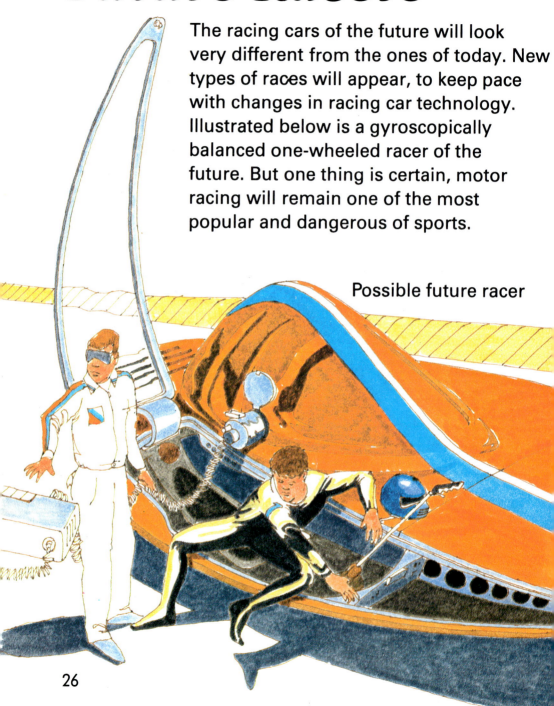

Possible future racer

How would gyroscopes balance the one-wheeled racer?

You've probably seen toy gyroscopes.. They have a large wheel that spins inside a fixed frame. This allows them to balance at almost any angle.

Do you have any ideas for future racers?

Answers

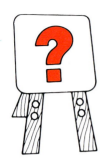

What fuel do today's racing cars use?

Grand Prix Cars use high octane gasoline. Alcohol and benzene fuels are used in some other forms of racing.

When was the first British Grand Prix?

In 1926, at the famous Brooklands racing circuit.

Can you name any other famous drivers of this period?

Achille Varzi was Nuvolari's great rival. Rudolf Caracciola and Sir Henry Segrave were other great drivers.

Can you name any Grand Prix races?

Grand Prix races are held in most European countries. There are also races in North and South America and Africa.

What is a turbocharged engine?

Turbocharged engines can be more powerful than engines twice their size. Exhaust gases from the engine are used to power turbines, that compress the fuel mixture before it enters the engine.

Can you name other Formulas?

Formula 2 and Formula 3 racing cars race in their own events. Other Formulas include Formula Ford and Formula 5000.

How did the pits get their name?

In the very early days of motor racing the pits were just that – pits dug beside the track, so that mechanics could work under the cars.

Why do spectators need protecting?

Spectators stand very close to the race track. A tragic accident during the Le Mans 24-hour race in 1955 killed 87 spectators when a car crashed and plunged into the crowd.

When is the Indianapolis 500 run?

Each year on the anniversary of the first Indianapolis 500 in 1911 – the 30th of May.

When was the first Le Mans 24-hour race?

The first race was in 1923.

Index

WITHDRAWN